How To Flip
Your First House

The Beginner's Guide To House Flipping

Jeff Leighton

Table of Contents

A Note To
The Future House Flipper

This book will help you flip your first house – fast. Whether you've looked at a few properties already or not, this book is a recipe for your first successful flip. Believe it or not – there is a process and a formula to flipping houses that can be followed by anyone. There is a system behind this business and a system behind doing your first deal.

Over the last several years I have flipped numerous houses and worked with some of the top real estate investors in the world. I have implemented the secrets they shared with me into my own business.

This is not a theory book. Everything in here has been tested by myself or an investor friend whom I know, like, and trust. I have seen numerous part-time investors make the transition to full-time after learning these strategies. In this book we will go over real-life examples and a step-by-step process to make sure your first flip is a success. That will then open the doors to more flips and even to quitting your job and doing this full-time.

Flipping is one of the oldest businesses in the world: buying an asset at a low price, fixing it up, and then selling it at a higher price. You can see this business model in nearly any industry since the beginning of time.

The business will always be around because there will always be motivated sellers, no matter what the economy is doing or what a CNN or Fox News headline says. At any given point you go to any city in America and find renovated properties by investors, many of whom are just regular people who have learned how to find deals, fix houses, and make large profits doing so.

The great thing about getting into this business and doing your first flip is that you can start part-time and eventually, after you have done a couple of successful flips, then transition into a full-time real estate investor. In this book we just focus on your first flip, although the income potential in this business is unlimited. I know some people that flip a couple of houses a year, and some that do several a month and then move up to larger-scale projects and luxury flips. It's completely up to you.

Each chapter contains action steps that you can implement in your own business. The more action you take, the faster you will see results and the sooner you can complete your first successful flip. In the next chapter I'll start by telling you the very first thing you need to do to ensure a successful flip.

CHAPTER 1

Get Educated With
Insider Information

The most important thing you need to do before getting into real estate investing and flipping your first house is becoming educated. Now, the great thing about flipping houses is that you do not need any type of formal degree like a college or master's degree. In fact, looking back on what I know now, I would have spent my college years learning the specialized information about house flipping and not the general info you learn in college. There are several ways to learn this specialized info, all of which I have done and listed below.

First of all, you should familiarize yourself and listen to as many real estate investing podcasts as possible. For starters, they are free and easy to listen to when you are driving around. Even if you just get one thing from each interview, you will learn a ton about real estate investing. On these podcasts, full-time real estate investors are interviewed and go over everything from their favorite marketing strategies, to what kinds of deals they are doing, to their own stories of getting started in real estate investing. These days there are so many good real estate investing podcasts out there. I would say, check out the BiggerPockets podcast, Best Ever Show, Real Estate Investing Mastery, and so many others.

The next great place to start learning are books on house flipping on Amazon, such as the one you are reading now. Go through several books, since each house flipper is in a different area and may have a slightly different strategy. Look for the commonalities that the different house flippers may have so that you can develop your own strategy. For instance, some investors may be in very high-end areas and some may be in very low-end areas, but maybe they both do a lot of direct mailing. That is probably something you would want to incorporate into your business.

Another place to get started with real estate investing is working for a local house flipper on a part-time or even full-time basis. There are several ways to set this up. Number one, if you are going to REIA (Real Estate Investor Association) meetings or Meetup groups for real estate investors – which you should be doing –, there are tons of networking opportunities that can open up doors to part-time or full-time positions. All you have to do is ask. Additionally, if you go to the Craigslist jobs section in your area, there are always part-time and full-time positions that local real estate developers and house flippers will post on there, since we are always looking for good people to work with.

Social media is another way. If you follow some of the top real estate investors on their social media profiles, they will often say, "We're hiring" an acquisitions person, a lead manager, a project manager, a marketing specialist, etc. Another great way of working with local house flippers is to just start doing marketing and bringing them your best leads. When I first got started doing my own marketing, I would bring the best leads to a local investor who very much appreciated me doing this and would then help me put the deals together. He got free leads from me and was able to do more deals, and I was able to see how he closed the deals and how he worked, so it was a win-win situation. We will go in depth later on in this book on how to generate off market leads but keep in mind that most of the top investors in your area will have joint venture programs for newer investors where you just have to bring them the good leads and they will do the rest of the work for you.

One of the best way and most overlooked ways to get an education in real estate investing is to join a coaching program and get a real estate millionaire as your mentor – which is what I did. The coaching program I joined was expensive – and still is – but if you are serious about this business and want the best education possible, then I would recommend joining one. When you pay for something, especially when it costs more than $10, it forces you to take action. You put a lot into it, so you value it much more. I never would have had the drive to succeed as much if I hadn't made a large investment in my personal education. Also, the great thing about coaching programs is that you learn the correct way of doing real estate investing and you are surrounded by a group of other committed real estate investment professionals. You can bounce ideas off of more successful investors and see what has been successful for other students in the program. Moreover, there are countless networking opportunities when you join a coaching. If you want to learn more about the coaching program I am still a member of, then check out my website www.MasteryCoachingWithJeff.com, watch the free video, and submit your contact information to find out whether it is a good fit for you.

Overall, when you are getting started in real estate investing, you should do a combination of all the ideas mentioned above. You should immerse yourself in podcast interviews to model the successful investors, read books about the best strategies for real estate investing, work either part-time or full-time with other local real estate investors, and make the commitment to join a coaching program so that you surround yourself with other people who have the same goals and dreams.

CHAPTER 2

Types of Flipping To Maximize Profit

When we talk about flipping your first house, keep in mind that you can use several exit strategies for your first flip. You should focus on one of the strategies when starting out and become an expert in that niche. Starting out with the goal being a year or two from now, you could utilize all of the exit strategies and become a transaction engineer. The three main ones are rehabbing, wholesaling, and wholetaling. We will go over each one.

Rehabbing is the most common strategy to flipping a house. You buy the house, fix it up, and then resell it. This is usually the most profitable of the three strategies, but also the riskiest and most time-intensive one. It can also be the most rewarding, however, when you see a property transform from a fixer upper to the nicest house in the neighborhood. With rehabbing, you need to keep in mind that it can take several months to fix up the property and then several more months to sell it, so it's not as fast as other types of investment deals such as a wholesale deal. When doing your first rehab project, I usually recommend you start with a smaller project instead of a complete teardown of a house.

Real estate wholesaling is a great strategy for beginners in real estate investing. Even if you prefer fixing up and doing the development aspect of real estate, I would recommend that you learn wholesaling, mainly because you are learning how to generate consistent investment leads. Wholesaling is the least risky of the investment strategies and also the fastest way to get paid on a deal. With wholesaling you are finding off-market properties that could be good deals for investors, and then assigning the rights of that contract to the investor for a fee. You need to be able to find leads as well as have a team of investor buyers ready to purchase your deals. One tip for newer investors is to focus on generating leads from off-market sellers. Then, when you get a good lead or two, you can often send that lead over to the top wholesaler in your area and work together to get the deal sold. The top wholesalers usually have massive buyer lists of investors and often offer joint venture possibilities to newer investors. We will go into more strategies on how to find deals and investors in the next chapter.

Wholetaling or "prehabbing" is another good option for real estate investors that carries less risk than a rehab and has more profit potential than a wholesale deal. Wholetaling gives you the best of both worlds when it comes to investing. With wholetaling you purchase the property, but you don't do an extensive renovation like you would with a rehab. You fix it up enough so that it can be financed by a traditional buyer or an investor. This means removing any junk in the house, fixing any drastic issues such as a roof leak or missing appliances, some landscaping to improve the curb appeal, and then putting it up for sale. Since you list the property on the MLS in "as is" condition, you will have potentially thousands more people looking at the home than you would if you just sent it out to your buyer's list. Once you start doing more deals, wholetaling can be a great option because you might be busy with other projects and not have the time or resources to do a full renovation. Overall, wholetaling should be part of every real estate investor's tool kit when it comes to different exit strategies.

Refer it out. Sometimes, when you are getting started in real estate, you may come across a unique type of property that is out of your wheelhouse. This could be a potential land development, commercial property, or even a condo conversion. In these scenarios, it is much more difficult to come up with a price to pay since you don't have that type of experience. What I typically do with these properties is refer them to investors who specialize in those types of deals. From going to REIA meetings or just a basic search online, you should be able to find people that specialize in the type of deal that you have come across. If it's a good deal, they should be able to pay you some type of referral or assignment fee. They appreciate you sending them leads and will likely reciprocate down the road at some point and send you some leads as well. I like to view all of my so-called competition as partners. Doing that can open up a whole new world of joint venture possibilities.

Keep in mind that we just covered four of the main exit strategies – believe it or not, there are even more than that. Some of the more advanced strategies include lease options, seller financing, buy and hold, and 1031 exchanges. Each area also has different publicly available zoning laws, which can give you a huge advantage and allow you to see potential deals that no one else saw because you know the zoning. The great thing about real estate investing is that once you get into the business, start getting leads, and do your first deal, you will start to realize which strategy suits you best, and you will get better and evolve with every deal. Every real estate investor I know has their own little niche. The more you learn and take action, the sooner you will find your place in this business.

CHAPTER 3

Easy-To-Implement Marketing To Find Deals

Being able to find deals as an investor is the most important aspect of this business. In this chapter, we will go over the top ways to consistently find deals. The best investors I know are all lead generation experts who use multiple strategies to find deals. We will go over those strategies here. The key with finding deals is to cherry-pick the best ones. Ideally, you want to get so many leads that you have the luxury of only choosing the low-hanging fruit.

MLS: The first and most common way of finding your first flip is the MLS. If you don't have access to the MLS, I would link up with a real estate agent who can either give you their access or set you up with an automated search. Many investors have a search set up that notifies them every day if a property gets listed and has keywords in the listing such as "fixer upper, estate sale, needs work, handyman special," and other things like that. You can also set it up to automatically send you deals by price point and neighborhood. Since so many people have access to the MLS, you need to move very quickly if you come across a deal you think has potential. Most of the investment properties out there are on the MLS, so this can be a great free place to start. Also, keep in mind that MLS is great for rehabs, I would not recommend wholesaling an MLS deal when you are getting started.

Wholesalers: The next strategy you should utilize, no matter what market you are in, is working with wholesalers. If you are very new to real estate investing, a wholesaler is a type of investor who will do the work of finding a deal and will sell you the rights to a fixer upper property for a fee of anywhere from 5K to 50K. The idea is that a wholesaler will serve you up a deal on a silver platter without you having to do any legwork of finding the property. Now, wholesalers often send out deals that don't quite meet the criteria you are looking for. However, those deals are typically off-market and sometimes have potential. The key to working with wholesalers is to try to build a whole team of wholesalers instead of just relying on one or two. Ideally, you want 10-25 wholesalers sending you leads on a consistent basis because chances are that maybe only one or two leads in ten will be a good lead. The way to build your team of wholesalers is to write down any bandit sign number you see, attend as many real estate investing networking meetings as you can, and even search websites like LinkedIn. You can type in "wholesaler", click on your city and the real estate industry, and there should be at least 25 results, depending on how large your city is. I know investors who rely solely on wholesalers to bring them deals, so this should definitely be part of your initial strategy since it is free.

Real estate agents: Real estate agents are also a great source of leads for potential flips.

Similar to wholesalers, for this marketing strategy to be effective you need a whole team of real estate agents bringing you off-market deals that are not yet listed, as well as deals on the MLS that they might have an inside scoop on. Since you are an investor, I would not recommend signing a buyer's agent agreement with an agent. Instead, if you buy a house from them, tell them they can list the property once it's fixed up. Getting both sides of the commission should motivate them enough to start finding you deals. I know an investor who does this successfully and has made a list of every single real estate agent who has done a deal in the last six months in our area. He called, emailed, and texted about 500 agents, letting them know he was an investor and that if they came across a good deal, he would be interested and they could list it once the house was renovated. As a result of this strategy he built a solid team of 25 or so real estate agents that now scour the city looking for deals for him. His pipeline is always full. The moral of the story: don't just rely on one agent, but try to build a team.

Direct mail: Direct mail is my favorite way of finding deals because it is so targeted, scalable, and fairly easy to run once you have set up your system. I like to mail to absentee owners, eviction, probate, and other types of motivated sellers. There are really about 20 different groups of motivated sellers out there in any city in the US, including pre-foreclosure, delinquent property taxes, inherited homes, high equity owners, and more. The reason I like to direct mail so much is that you can start by sending out a small number of letters or postcards, and once you get a hang of it, you can scale it up. I even know investors that mail out 10,000 postcards a month, knowing they will get anywhere from 150 to 200 leads, which should lead to at least three or four houses to flip. I even read an interview with some of the top investors across the country who said that, if they had $500 or $5,000 to spend on marketing, direct mail would be their main source of marketing. I like to think of direct mail like the movie *Moneyball* with Brad Pitt except that it's for real estate investing. What I mean is, with direct mail you can become a data analytics expert and only market to the potentially motivated sellers in your city, uncovering diamonds in the rough properties that nobody else knows about. There are numerous places to find these motivated seller lists, including online at your courthouse records. You can also purchase these lists inexpensively in places like ListSource.com or AlescoData.com. Once you have your list, all you have to do is mail it out. There are literally tons of places that will mail out your list for you. My favorite one is www.Click2Mail.com. Direct mail is the best way to uncover high profit off market properties that you can wholesale or rehab.

Internet marketing: Online marketing has become a popular source of finding deals, although it is a more advanced strategy. There are a lot of investors that will do AdWords or pay per click to find deals, which works very well for them. AdWords is similar to direct mail but online, because again it is very targeted. You can set it up so that only people in your area who type in phrases on Google such as "sell my house fast" and similar terms will see your ad. If you are more technology-inclined, this can be a great way to generate leads and deals. I would recommend spending $20 and getting any book by Perry Marshall on AdWords, since this is a more complicated strategy to get into. You can also model the top investors in your area doing similar ads when you are first getting started. Or even see what the top companies in other cities do for their AdWords campaigns. Just type in "we buy houses" for a city other than yours, see what comes up, and then model that for your first AdWords campaign.

I think every real estate investor should go to at least a couple of real estate auctions just to see how they operate. However, it is not my favorite place for finding deals, and I would not recommend auctions for beginners. Usually, the people buying houses at auctions have been doing it for years and pay cash out of their own pocket for each house. Most of the time they are not able to view the property before buying it, so they take a lot of risk. Auctions are definitely an interesting place to go to, usually taking place on the steps of the courthouse, but I don't think they are the best for deals. You can use them to gain more knowledge about the business, as well as to get some business cards from the cash buyers who are down there.

Bandit signs are a tried-and-true marketing strategy to generate leads. They are inexpensive: they usually cost $2 or $3, you can purchase them online, and they are very simple. The signs should just have your phone number on them, along with "We Buy Houses". You should always check with your local county to make sure you are allowed to put them up. You should put the signs up in high-traffic areas, i.e. not far out in the suburbs where two cars may drive by in a given day. Bandit signs are a little more time-intensive than some of the other forms of marketing like direct mail, so ideally, you should outsource this to a local person as soon as you can. One investor who does really well with bandit signs created a route on Google Maps to indicate where exactly each sign should go. He then drove the route himself to see how long it takes and outsourced it to a local person who puts up the signs once a week. Now, this investor has 25 signs that go up each week for $100 a month and he has created a nice marketing system for himself.

Another inexpensive yet proven form of marketing would be "We Buy Houses" car magnets. I know many investors who consistently get leads and deals from this strategy. You can buy these car magnets for under $20 and put them on your car or even pay other people to put them on their cars. The sign is very simple and just says "We Buy Houses" and then has a local phone number that a potential seller can call. If you are driving around a city a lot this can be a great strategy. You can also just park your car in a high traffic area for the day and see what type of leads come in. Some investors will purchase a large truck on Craigslist or elsewhere and put their "We Buy Houses" sign on the truck and then just pay a local gas station or other business to park their car in a high visibility area.

Overall, with your real estate marketing, you should start with one of the strategies mentioned above and become a master of that. Once you know how to generate leads, you should expand eventually to where you have at least three viable strategies that are bringing in leads and deals. You never want to rely on just one marketing strategy in this business. The top investors in this game usually all have a solid direct mail campaign, lots of online marketing, and are well connected with local real estate agents and wholesalers who regularly send them off market deals. Think of your marketing like a military-style attack coming from the air, land, and sea. To flip your first house you will need to get a minimum of 25 leads and sometimes even more than that for your first deal. Most of your leads will not be great but out of 25 leads there should be a couple motivated sellers who are looking to sell ASAP and at a good price. Also, once you start getting all these leads, you will need some type of system to handle all the phone calls. I have all my leads outsourced to a live call-answering service, and then I only follow up with the motivated sellers, which saves me a ton of time. The best call-answering services out there for real estate investors include PAT Live and Answer First. Both are fairly inexpensive.

CHAPTER 4

Tactics For Making Offers

When you are first getting started, making an offer can be intimidating. However, after a couple of times, you will be a pro. Below is my three-step system for making offers, which makes things simple and easy. Before you start making offers, I would always recommend familiarizing yourself with your area and looking at the prices of at least 100 houses online so that you can get a general idea of what places sell for renovated vs non-renovated. Sometimes neighborhoods can vary drastically just one block from the next.

Keep in mind that, depending on your jurisdiction, there are different types of standard contracts. If you want to see the one I use, you can email info@actionhomebuyers.com to get an idea. I would always recommend that you run any contract by a lawyer; however, I have had success with it in three different states without issues. The contract I use is simple and is not a 40-page real estate agent contract, which are fairly common these days if you work with an agent. That is why I recommend starting with off-market properties: if you use a standard contract with a real estate agent, it can be long and intimidating. Once you have your contract ready, you should familiarize yourself with it and even practice filling it out a couple of times so that you know what you are doing.

After you have your purchase and sale agreement ready to go, you should only make offers to motivated sellers. Keep in mind that if you start doing marketing and generating leads, most of your leads won't be motivated. There might only be one or two in ten leads that are worth following up with. Most sellers that call you will say, "I want to sell my house for 1 million dollars. I am going to list it with a real estate agent, but I just wanted to give you a shot at it." Those are not the people you should be making offers to. The only people you should make offers to are motivated sellers. A motivated seller is someone that says, "My house needs a lot of work. I want to sell it ASAP."

Now that you have your contract down and you have found a motivated seller, the next step is to use the MAO formula for making an offer. The MAO formula is a common real estate investing term that states that your maximum allowable offer or MAO should equal the renovated value times .7

minus the cost of repairs. You should write this down and use it as a standard system for any offers. Here it is again: MAO = ARV * .7 – the cost of repairs. If a property sells for 200K renovated and needs 40K worth of work, then the MAO would be 200 times .7 minus 40K, which would give you 100K as your maximum allowable offer. I know that sounds low as an offer price, but that margin is what ensures you make a nice profit. In some cases, it does make sense to offer more than the .7 ARV amount, for example if the property does not need a lot of work and the houses sell very quickly in that neighborhood so there is less risk. The opposite is also true: if the property needs a lot of work and is in a not so great neighborhood, then you may want to be closer to .6 or .65 ARV on your offer. Sometimes it is hard to find properties that meet the MAO formula so that is why I recommend working with a top local investor for your first deal. If you get any lead that you think has any amount of potential then you can send that lead over to the top investor. The top investor will often have a buyers list of thousands of people and chances are they will have someone that is interested in buying it at a price above the MAO formula. In a good market, as long as you find deals that are less than what they would sell for listed on the MLS with an agent then you can wholesale it. The best way to find the top investor in your area is to see which company is advertising everywhere, which company is everyone talking about? Go to your local REIA, search online for we buy houses companies in your area, ask real estate agents, ask other investors, and go to Meetup groups. I can guarantee you that you will start to hear the same names over and over again and those are the people you should be working with.

CHAPTER 5

No Nonsense
Mistakes To Avoid

In this chapter we will go over the top 10 mistakes that I see newer investors make. If I'd known what I know now when I first started, it could have saved me a lot of headaches. In other words, don't hesitate to read this chapter several times. It will be worth your while.

1. *Getting Advice From the Wrong People*

    I could probably write a whole book on why you need to be very careful about who you get advice from, but I will try to keep it shorter. If you tell people that you will start flipping houses or get started in real estate investing, they will tell you every reason under the sun why you should not. The only problem is the people telling you this don't want to see you succeed and are often unsuccessful themselves. Here are some specific examples of people you should not listen to.

    - Your local know-it-all real estate agent

        Let me start by pointing out there are many great real estate agents out there that love to work with investors and understand the business. However, I think we all know at least one "know-it-all real estate agent" who does not like investing and has never been successful in investing. Every area has one or several of these agents that can give you every reason why house flipping does not work. The only problem is, they have never done a successful deal. In fact, they often tried house flipping at one point in their career and failed miserably. As a result, they still have a bad taste in their mouth. Stay away from these people and take everything they say with a grain of salt.

    - CNN or Fox News headlines

        It seems like every week there is a new stat or dramatic headline about house flipping, usually on one of the big news networks. Sometimes they say house flipping is back, and sometimes house flipping is dead. Either way, the news is often reported by someone who is not a full-time house flipper and really has no idea what they are talking about. At any point in the economy you could cherry-pick various stats that could make it seem like house flipping is back or house flipping is dead. Stats lie and can be manipulated to support any argument, so try to stay away from those dramatic clickbait headlines you might see on the news or online.

- <u>Friends and family members</u>
This one is harder because friends or family members can have a negative outlook on house flipping. They may say it's too risky, they may say it's a scam, they will ask you why you don't just work a normal, steady job with a consistent paycheck. I've heard all of these. When you get into this business, you have to think about your goals and stay focused. Don't listen to people who try to discourage you from becoming an investor.

To reiterate this point, here are examples of people you *should* listen to.

- <u>Successful investors that are interviewed on podcasts, YouTube, and elsewhere</u>
These days there are tons of great podcasts out there that interview successful investors from across the country doing different types of deals in different types of markets. Some of the podcasts include *BiggerPockets, Best Ever Show, Epic Real Estate*, and many more. All of these people are full-time real estate investors who worked other jobs before making the jump into real estate investing. You can learn a lot from their stories and theirs trials and tribulations.

- <u>Full-time house flippers that you meet at REIA meetings or in Meetup groups</u>
The person running your local REIA or various people you may meet at one of these real estate investing associations are often full-time house flippers. They can share insights and in some cases even offer different opportunities to work together and partner with local investors getting started. A full-time real estate investor

that you meet in a REIA or Meetup group, especially a local one, will have a very different opinion on real estate investing than a CNN headline or a jaded real estate agent. I can guarantee it.

- Coaching or mentoring programs

    When I first got started in real estate investing, I joined a coaching program. Although it was expensive, it was one of the best decisions I've ever made. There is a whole world of real estate investing and house flipping that 99% of the population does not even know about. Gaining this specialized info from a coaching program put me much further ahead of the competition. The people who start these programs have often done hundreds, if not thousands, of real estate deals and are the best at what they do. If you want more information on the coaching program I joined, then check out www.MasteryCoachingWithJeff.com, watch the free video, and fill out the form to learn more.

2. *Getting in Over Your Head*

    I have talked to literally hundreds if not thousands of newer investors who have never flipped a house before. Occasionally they will ask me about a lead they are working on that involves knocking down a house and subdividing three lots or building a new construction. My first response is, "Why in the world would you want to do that as your first deal?" Building a house, much less subdividing a property, is something that even some developers who have been in the business for over ten years and who have done hundreds of deals don't do. Unless you come from a construction background, when you are getting started with your first deal, I would recommend choosing a simpler project, i.e. a house that just needs cosmetic work or just wholesaling a deal to a more experienced investor. The thing with investing is that projects almost always cost more and take longer than anticipated. That is why you need to start small with something manageable. Townhouses, condos, or small single-family houses work great for your first deal. Stay away from properties that need large additions, new construction, or complete gut jobs.

3. *Weird Houses*

Sometimes investors want to get my opinion on deals they are looking at, but then they send me what I consider "weird houses". Weird houses to me are houses that fit a couple of different requirements. For starters, they may be unusually small for the neighborhood and, therefore, unusually low-priced. While it may look like a good deal if a house is unusually small for the area, I need to see at least a couple of sold houses that are of the same size. Just because the price is significantly lower does not mean it's a good deal. A house that small will take a lot longer to sell and will sell for a lot less than the neighborhood.

Another characteristic of weird houses is teardowns. You can come across these uninhabitable teardown houses in many neighborhoods, and you should be careful because they will sell for significantly less than other homes and could skew your comps. The best way to get a good idea of what these teardowns are worth is to look at any new construction homes in your area and what price the builder paid for the house. You should see a trend of what builders pay for teardown houses in your area. If you are still unsure, then you can ask a more experienced investor and possibly partner on the deal. Anytime I come across a deal that is over my head I present the deal to a trustworthy and more experienced partner who lets me know what I should do with it. Usually, we end up splitting it.

Lastly, the third characteristic of weird houses is that they are often located right on a busy road or in front of a large landmark, like a school. I try to avoid houses on busy roads and in front of schools, gas stations, fire stations, or any type of large landmark besides a park. While there are certainly exceptions, you need to factor in a much lower price for houses on busy roads and only use comps that sold on that busy road. Houses just one block away on a quieter street have a very different value. Whatever you do, make sure not to buy a house on a busy road, in front of a school, in teardown condition.

4. *Partnering With the Wrong People*

For your first couple of deals, I would recommend doing the deal just by yourself or with a more experienced full-time investor. The likelihood of deals going bad is higher you're new to the game, so I would avoid working with friends or family until you have more experience. When you are first getting started, it is very tempting to partner with everyone on your deal. However, I would be very careful about it, especially with your first deal. The bottom line is: never jump into any business relationship full-time. Start with smaller items, and then scale up if you see fit. There can be amazing relationships and not so amazing ones, so always start small, and make sure the person has a good reputation and that you know them well.

5. *Not Evaluating Enough Deals*

People often ask me what I think about a house right next door to them. They think it's a deal just because it's for sale, or maybe it looks vacant and appears to be a good prospect for a flip. I always tell new investors that they should see at least 100 houses before they buy their first flip. Now, you don't necessarily need to drive to 100 houses and go inside each one, but run 100 different houses through your deal analyzer so that you have an idea of what price point a good deal is. Keep in mind that most houses are not good deals. Just because your neighbor's house is for sale does not mean it is a good flip opportunity. As an investor, you really have to qualify and cherry-pick the best deals.

6. *Overpaying for Houses*

Newer buyers often assume they would make a profit if they bought a house at 200K, just because another house in their neighborhood sold for 300K. While that could be true, you need a better formula than that. You need to have a deal analyzer, which you can get by emailing us at <u>info@actionhome</u>
<u>buyers.com</u>. A deal analyzer qualifies the deal and shows you exactly how much you could make on it, taking into account holding costs, commissions, and repair costs, and using a conservative after repair value or ARV.

Another way to quickly tell if it's a good deal or not is using the MAO formula, or maximum allowable offer, which states that your maximum allowable offer should be the after repair value times .7 minus the cost of repairs. We have a whole chapter on evaluating deals, but you need to use the MAO formula on all deals.

Lastly, if you don't have a deal analyzer and you don't use the MAO formula, at the very least there should be a big difference between what you are paying for the house and what the Zillow value is. For example, these are the last two houses I bought: for one house, the Zillow value was 240K, and I bought it for 115K. The other house's Zillow value was 625K, and I bought it for 350K.

7. *Not Following a Proven Formula*

Take marketing for deals as an example. I always recommend the tried-and-true marketing strategies of direct mail, bandit signs, MLS searches, strategic networking, car magnets, and online marketing for investors who are just getting started. Choose one, get a couple of leads, and then grow it from there. However, you would not believe how many people will try some pie-in-the-sky marketing strategy that I've never heard of. One investor I recently consulted with told me he had paid a grocery store for thousands of ads on grocery carts. Now, while I am always to open to trying new marketing strategies, why would you ever try something like that as your first marketing campaign? Last time I checked, there were not thousands of articles and trainings on how to market correctly at grocery stores, and probably for a good reason. Stick with the proven strategies first, and then venture onto the other types.

8. *Expecting the Market to Increase*

When you are buying houses, you need to assume that the market will stay where it is currently at. If properties have sold for 200K renovated over the past year, then that is the number you need to use in your analysis. You should not factor in any type of increase in sales price because you think the market will go up. With flipping, you never buy for appreciation. If it happens, then that's a bonus, but never factor it into your equation. That is how a lot of people got in trouble with the market crash of 2008: they just assumed that property values would keep inflating, until it was too late.

9. *Not Evaluating Repairs Correctly*

With real estate investing it is best to systematize everything. When it comes down to evaluating repairs, that is no different. You need a repair estimator (which I have a link to at the end of this book) that can give you a good estimate of what repairs cost.

Depending on where you live, repairs will be different, so you need a couple strategies to decide repair costs. For starters, there is a free website called HomeAdvisor.com, which can tell you exactly what it costs based on your zip code for different home repairs. It even gives you a low estimate, a medium estimate, and a high estimate for different repairs.

Next, you should be talking to other real estate investors and looking at as many case studies as you can about what they are paying to renovate properties. You can do that at local REIAs and Meetup groups.

The key to a repair estimate is not to be 100% accurate but to be in the ballpark. If you think a house needs 25K worth of work, but it really needs 50K, then your budget will be completely screwed up. With the repair estimator I use, I put in all the repairs, and it automatically adds 10% to any repair budget, just to be conservative. That will make your evaluations much more accurate.

10. *Focusing on Too Many Exit Strategies*

When you are getting started, you should already have in mind what you are looking to do – whether that is rehabbing it, wholesaling, or buying and holding. Your exit strategy will determine how you go about finding properties. For example, if you are looking to rehab, then you should look on the MLS, do direct marketing, networking, and online advertising. However, if you are only wholesaling, for example, then should only be looking at off market properties from leads that you generate, (i.e. do not look on the MLS for wholesale deals).

Choose your strategy, get a couple of deals done that way, and then expand on your exit strategies. Like I've said before, most of the best investors will have several different exit strategies. At any given time they may be working on a couple of rehabs, wholesaling a deal, and own several rental properties that generate cash flow every month.

CHAPTER 6

Strategies To Fund Your Deal

Funding your deal is the most important part of real estate investing if you are doing a rehab. Fortunately, there are several ways to get funding, even if you don't have any money yourself.

The first way is something a lot of real estate investors use: hard money. Hard money is short-term loans for investors that charge anywhere from 12 to 15% and 2-5 points. Although it sounds expensive, a good hard money lender can typically fund your deal in as little as a week or ten days. The reason real estate investors pay more for this type of money is that it is fast and flexible. In most scenarios, a hard money lender funds 65% ARV, which means that, even with the best deals, you still have to bring some money to the table, usually at least 10%. However, many investors I know have another friend or associate who provides those funds. We talk about how to find the best hard money lenders in another chapter; however, keep in mind that each hard money lender will offer different rates and have different ways of doing business, so it's important to reach out to several of them to get an idea.

Partnering is another option, but it is the most expensive one. Nevertheless, many people do this when they are getting started since they don't have the track record yet. Partnering is exactly what it sounds like: you find a partner – maybe a friend or real estate associate – who has the money and you decide on what your partnership should be. Sometimes it is 50/50, and sometimes it might be 60/40. It is completely up to you and what you think is fair. Usually, one person will find and manage the deal, while the other person will fund it and possibly take more risk. After doing a deal or two this way, ideally, you would want to evolve to a less expensive type of funding, such as hard money, and eventually private money.

Private money is the least expensive and most flexible form of funding. This is what your eventual goal should be: to have enough private lenders so that you can have as many projects as you can handle every month. Private money works like this: your investor will completely or partially fund your deal and rehab costs. They are essentially the bank, and in exchange for borrowing the money, you will sign a promissory note and a mortgage note that secures their funds to the property. Private money is a great alternative to a traditional bank, which can take forever, as well as hard money, which can be much more expensive. The best thing about private money is that it is completely negotiable for you and your investor. I see many private money loans at around 10-12% with zero points, as opposed to the 12-15% and two to five points you might see with hard money. The way you find private money lenders is by building relationships with other real estate professionals and other professionals. Your private money lenders might often come through referrals from other investors, agents, or even friends and family. Your end goal should be to build up a roster of private money lenders that you can draw from at any time instead of just relying on one or two. Often, once you have done one successful deal with a private money lender, they will be lining up to do a second deal with you and tell everyone they know about it.

Conventional financing is the most common way to go when you are purchasing a property. In some cases you can even finance your first flip this way. Banks are a lot more strict than a hard money lender or private money lender, so if you are looking to finance your first flip with a conventional loan, then the property cannot be in too bad a shape. However, you can find plenty of homes that are in original condition and just need some sprucing up. Banks typically won't loan conventional financing on properties that need extensive work, such as homes that have roof leaks and foundation issues, for example. In general, all major systems, such as HVAC, electrical, and plumbing, need to be in working condition. Buying a fixer upper with conventional financing can be a great way to get started, and you could even live in the property and rent out a room or two to pay for some of the upgrades and save money.

In this chapter we covered several different ways of financing your first flip, including hard money, private money, partnerships, and conventional financing. You should be familiar with all of these ways of financing because they all have their time and place in the real estate investing world. I know plenty of investors who may have one deal going with hard money, one with private money, and possibly even a partnership going – all at the same time. Do what works for you when you are getting started. Your long-term goal should be to use a combination of mostly private money (the least expensive) and hard money (the most flexible).

CHAPTER 7

Savvy Ways To
Build Your Team

When you are starting out in real estate investing, you need to think of your business as a team, as if you are creating the Dream Team of real estate investing. Some of the major players on your team should include real estate agents, wholesalers, contractors, title companies, and hard money lenders. You will also add other people to your team, and I would recommend keeping everyone in a database, or at the very least, an Excel spreadsheet.

Finding Title Companies

Finding a good title company is a lot easier than it used to be. If you've never bought a house before, a title company is where you go to sign the paperwork to purchase or sell the home. Thanks to the market crash of 2008, a lot of the bad apples were weeded out, including some title companies. Nowadays, the process of closing is very regulated, and companies that are not performing will be out of business.

The best place to find an investor-friendly title company is through referrals from other investors and real estate agents. You can call and ask title companies if they are investor-friendly, like I did when I was getting started. However, I can assure you they will say yes regardless of whether or not they work with a lot of investors, since they don't want to turn down business. It's best to get a couple of referrals for title companies and try out several before deciding on which one you want to use.

Keep in mind as well that other investors do not mind sharing this resource with you. In some cases, they might even get discounts on their future deals by referring as many people as possible. So be sure to ask as many real estate professionals as possible about their preferred title companies, because you will start to hear some of the same names over and over again. Those names are the people you want to work with.

Finding Hard Money Lenders

Having a good hard money lender on your team can be the difference between getting deals done and not. A hard money lender is the person that will lend you the majority of the money for your flip deal, so you need them to be responsive and easy to work with. It is very important that you find a couple of highly reputable hard money lenders that have been in business for a while and have good reviews.

When getting started, keep in mind that every city has anywhere from 10 to 100 hard money lenders operating in that area. Each hard money lender has a slightly different way of doing business and will charge you different amounts as well. Usually, once you have done a deal or two with a hard money lender, they will lower their rates. The first deal is usually the highest rate: somewhere in the range of 15% and two to five points on your money. Some hard money lenders even offer joint venture opportunities or might be willing to wholesale your deal since they have such a huge buyers list.

The best way to find hard money lenders is first doing an online search of hard money lenders in your city. After building a list of 10-20, you should start looking at their reviews and checking out their websites. Just from doing that, you should be able to tell who is more legitimate than others. You can then reach out and talk to them about how they work, and let them know you are a newer investor looking to build a long-term relationship. You should also be networking at REIAs and real estate Meetup groups, where other investors will tell you who they prefer over others. Sometimes the REIAs or Meetup groups are sponsored by hard money lenders so that is another way to find them. You ideally want to have at least three solid hard money lenders that you trust and that get good reviews or come recommended.

Finding Wholesalers

Wholesalers can be a beneficial and important part of your real estate investing team. The reason is that they will essentially bring you off-market real estate opportunities for free. The key to working with wholesalers when you are getting started is to have a lot of them on your team. By "team" I simply mean a list on an Excel spreadsheet or a database where you have their name, number, and any other information you care to input. You do not want to rely on just one wholesaler because wholesalers will often send you so-so deals or will not properly evaluate the repair budget.

You build up your list of wholesalers by going to REIA meetings and Meetup groups, writing down any number you see on bandit signs, and going on LinkedIn, typing in "wholesaler", and then going to your city. For each city there should be a list of at least ten or 25. If you eventually build up a list of 20 or even 50 wholesalers, then you can start to see tons of off-market leads and potentially buy one of them. I would look at wholesaler leads the same way you might look at any other lead: most are not good, but one or two in ten might have potential.

Finding Agents

When you first get started in real estate investing, I would recommend finding out who the investor-friendly agents in your area are. Eventually, you want to get your own license because it is not only surprisingly easy to get licensed, but it can also save you money down the road, since you can list your own properties or refer listings and buyers to full-time agents.

The best place to find investor-friendly agents is at local REIA and Meetup groups. You can also search online on websites like LinkedIn, where you can just type in "real estate agent" and click on your city. You should have several hundred agents show up, and then you can go through their profiles, see who would work with investors, and reach out. Also, everyone knows a friend or cousin who just got their license and can set you up on an automatic search for properties that need work. Tell them to set you up on a search for properties that meet certain keywords in the descriptions, such as "as is", "handyman special", "investors", "cash only", and other keywords.

I would not recommend signing any type of buyer agent agreement with a real estate agent because you are an investor. The investment deal could come from anywhere or anyone, so you don't want to be tied to one person. Any agent that does not understand that is someone you probably should not work with. Keep in mind that most agents do not work with investors, so you may have to go through five or ten agents to find an investor-friendly one.

Finding Contractors

When you are getting started as a real estate investor, finding a good contractor is of major importance. In this chapter we will go over three quick strategies that work in finding the best contractors.

Tip number one: Get a referral for a contractor from somebody in the business or someone that just had work done on their house. You can ask real estate agents, other investors, friends, or anybody you trust – ideally, someone in real estate. Most people don't have any issue whatsoever with recommending a contractor. It's even better if you can get a couple of referrals on contractors and then meet with three of them at a potential house you are looking at to see who would do the best job. Always do an online check of the contractor as well. Just because they are referred does not guarantee anything, although it does weed out a lot of bad contractors. Look online to make sure the contractor does not have bad reviews, and always make sure they have a license and insurance.

Tip number two: Go to the top real estate agent websites in your area and browse around. Typically, the top real estate agents will have a section on their website called "recommended vendors" or "recommended contractors". This is a gold mine, and you can build a substantial list of vetted contractors by going to a couple of these agents' sites. Once you have several names, you can cross-reference them with an online search of ratings/reviews to make sure they have a license and are insured.

Tip number three: Anytime you are driving around and see a house being renovated, you'll typically see a sign out front advertising their business (i.e. Bill's contractor services). Write down their name and number, or even take a photo of their sign so that you can add it to your list of contractors. You generally only want to hire "busy" contractors, since there is usually a reason they are busy. You should be wary of contractors that are not actively doing work.

By using these three strategies, you should be able to build up a large list of already vetted contractors in your area. Keep in mind too that some contractors will do a great job for a couple of projects and then start slacking off on the next ones, so that's why you always want to have several options. Also, I would always recommend starting on a smaller project first with your rehab deal. If it works out with that contractor, then consider doing larger projects.

CHAPTER 8

Advice For
Selling Your First Deal

I want to give you some strategies that would have saved me a lot of time and energy for when you sell your first deal. When starting out, you should do three things that will ensure a successful sale if you decide to do a rehab.

To start with, find a local reputable real estate agent who gets great reviews online and comes highly referred from a friend or another investor. You want to have a local agent who specializes in that area and has sold houses in that area before. I see people that try to either list the property themselves or just use an MLS placement service for which they might pay just $500 or so. I would advise against this because the property will sit on the market for months on end, the listing will become stale, and then you will start getting a lot of lowball offers. It's best to go with a professional who can get the job done from the start. They will be able to price the property correctly and make sure that it sells in a timely manner.

Secondly, make sure the real estate agent uses a professional photographer for their real estate listings. You want your property to be as presentable as possible, so paying a couple of extra hundred bucks to make your property look immaculate online is definitely worth it. These days everybody starts their real estate searches online. If your photos are not up to par, they will ignore your property and move on to the next one.

Lastly, I would recommend staging. Most people cannot envision how a property will look with furniture in it and think that rooms are much smaller than they are. Vacant houses can often seem cold and uninviting, so by having a good stager, you can warm your property up and make it much more presentable. About five years ago we never staged properties, but then we tried it a couple times and realized how much faster properties sell with good staging. Now we do it for nearly every property.

When it comes to rehabbing a house, If you have a good real estate agent who knows the market and lists your house at the correct price, professional photography, and a professional stager, the likelihood of your house selling quickly at a good price will be significantly higher.

It's Your Turn to Flip

After reading this book, you should have everything you need to start your first flip.

I purposely made this book short and straight to the point. I would even recommend reading it twice so you can internalize everything we have talked about here. If you follow the steps in this book, you will be ahead of 99% of the competition looking to get into flipping.

I wrote this book because I wanted to share the steps involved in your very first flip and explain what you need to know about real estate investing if you have never flipped before. It is an interesting and unique niche of business that can be mastered, just like any other skill.

There are full-time real estate investors in every market. By following the blueprint I have laid out, there is no reason why you cannot achieve that status sooner rather than later.

The first step is to take action, start marketing, and look for deals. Focus on one of the strategies we talked about — whether that's MLS searches, direct mail, bandit signs, car magnets, networking, or online marketing and just start generating leads. If there was one thing I could tell myself looking back to when I got started, it would be to become a lead generation master. If your phone is constantly ringing with sellers, you will always have opportunities to flip, even if you don't know a ton about real estate like I did when I was getting started.

There are countless examples of people who used to work full-time jobs that were not fulfilling. Through hard work, education, and taking action, they became successful full-time house flippers. By combining action-taking and consistently learning about the business, there is no way you cannot succeed.

I created this book so that you could successfully flip your first home, and then evolve beyond that into doing a couple of deals per year to eventually doing a couple of deals per month. The great thing about real estate investing is that with every deal you do, small or large, you become incrementally better and better.

It is now your turn to flip.

Thank you for getting my book! I really appreciate any feedback and would love to hear your opinion.

If you enjoyed this book, please leave me a helpful review on Amazon.

Thank you!

House-Flipping
Hacks for New Investors

I just wanted to throw in a list of the best house flipping hacks for new real estate investors that I could think of. We have already touched upon a couple of these, but I wanted you to have them in a list format so that you could refer to them when necessary.

1. For wholesaling your first deal, you can partner with more experienced investors. The top wholesalers in your area typically have thousands of people on their buyer lists. You can do a so-called "co-wholesale": they will send your deal out on their list to thousands of potential investors, and then you will split the deal. It's a great way to get your first deal done, since they will do most of the work, and you just have to find the good leads.

2. One of the best places to find good contractors is by browsing different local real estate agents' websites. They typically have a section on their site called "preferred vendors". You can start building a list of contractors from there and then cross-reference them with online reviews.

3. When you are not sure if a deal is good, the fastest way to tell is this. Go on Zillow and look at the Zestimate. There needs to be a big difference between the Zestimate and what the seller is looking to sell the house for. As an example, for the last two houses I bought, the Zestimate was about double of what I bought the property for. It doesn't always have to be that extreme, but if you think you might have a deal, always run it by another investor that you trust.

4. The best way to handle all the leads you get is a call-answering service. It is much less expensive than hiring an acquisitions person and will save you lots of time. For just a couple of hundred bucks a month you can have a full-time answering service, such as AnswerFirst or PAT Live, screening calls for you and sending you a text or email anytime

you get a lead. The top investors all use these types of services. They are easy to set up, you just give them a lead interview script where you ask the seller basic property info such as address, condition of house, and what price they are looking for.

5. You should listen to as many interviews of successful real estate investors as possible. The best way to do that is through freely available podcasts, such as Bigger Pockets, Best Ever Show, Epic Real Estate, and many others. There are plenty of apps, such as Stitcher, that you can download and listen to on 2X speed. In just one hour, you can probably listen to several investors' journeys to becoming an investor, the marketing strategies they use, as well as numerous other helpful tips.

6. If you are looking to build a list of real estate investors in your area for your buyers list or for research purposes, the most effective way is using LinkedIn. You can go on there, type in "real estate investor", and then click on your city. If you live in a large city, there should be hundreds of people that show up on that list. You can connect with them, or at least get their contact info, and start building your database.

7. If you have repetitive tasks that you would prefer to not do, then use a service such as Fiverr or Upwork. You can have a virtual assistant do various tasks for $5 or less an hour. This can be a great resource for things like building a list, researching properties, online marketing, and much more.

8. Learn the zoning laws of your area. This is a somewhat more advanced strategy, but most people in the real estate industry – including agents and other investors – have no idea about the zoning laws. If you spend some time reading the publicly available zoning laws from your county and city, you will start to see deals where others do not. I know that from first-hand experience: I sold a house that could have been converted into a five-unit condo building, and I lost out on a huge payday as a result of that. Then I became an expert!

9. If you can generate 50 leads a month, then you can be a full-time house flipper in any market. You need 50 leads because most leads are not motivated sellers, but one or two in ten leads will have potential. I stand by that statement. By 50 leads a month, I mean people calling you

directly from your direct mail, online marketing, or wholesalers bringing you off-market deals. The best way to get to 50 a month is to start by getting your first lead, then make it a goal to get ten leads a month, then 20, and you are on your way.

10. The best way to generate leads for your first flip – or any flip, for that matter – is direct mail. I personally use a service called www.click2mail.com to send out my mail, although there are probably hundreds of mail services out there. If you have never done a direct mail campaign, don't worry – you can use the exact same postcard that I use. See below, or feel free to email us at info@actionhomebuyers.com for a copy of it.

About the Author

Jeff Leighton is a real estate investor and agent who specializes in off-market properties. He has helped thousands of investors across the country find off-market deals in their own area and continues to invest successfully in a wide range of deals.

Resources and Next Steps

Want more next-level personalized real estate investing training? Here are some additional resources to help!

Join my email newsletter of weekly real estate investing tips. All you have to do is email "flip my first house" to info@actionhomebuyers.com to join the list and stay in touch.

Subscribe to my YouTube channel at www.youtube.com/jeffleighton, where I share weekly videos on real estate investing.

P.S. If you enjoyed this book I have a couple others below that offer a ton of value and are available on Amazon in kindle, paperback, or audiobook version, whichever you prefer.

21 Ways to Find Off-Market Deals: This book focuses on marketing for off market deals and goes over 21 proven strategies to finding those types of deals.

Probate Real Estate Investing: This book focuses on an overlooked and unique niche of real estate investing that has some of the best deals available in any market.

Off Market Real Estate Secrets: This book goes in depth on everything you need to know in the off market real estate world. It will open your eyes to deal-making possibilities.

I also do personalized coaching calls on a limited basis. If you are interested in booking a 30 minute 1 on 1 phone consultation then go here Clarity.fm/jeffleighton.

You can also join the same coaching program I joined when I got started with real estate investing at www.MasteryCoachingWithJeff.com.

I would love to stay in touch via social media, connect with me below.

YouTube -https://www.youtube.com/jeffleighton

Instagram -http://www.instagram.com/j_late12

Snapchat -https://www.snapchat.com/add/jrl560

Facebook -https://www.facebook.com/jeff.leighton.5

LinkedIn - http://www.linkedin.com/in/jeffleighton1

Made in the USA
Middletown, DE
27 January 2020